From
Nowhere to
Next

FROM NOWHERE TO NEXT

Startup Wisdom From Global Founders, Builders, and Innovators

Mehmet Gonullu

Published by Game Changer Publishing

Paperback ISBN: 978-1-968250-84-3
Hardcover ISBN: 978-1-968250-85-0
Digital ISBN: 978-1-968250-86-7

GAME CHANGER
PUBLISHING

www.GameChangerPublishing.com

I want to dedicate this book to my Dad and Mom,
who struggled a lot to get me to where I am today.

My wife, Humeyra, for her phenomenal support.

And my daughter, Yasmin, who was my source of inspiration.

Read This First

It means a lot that you're reading my book. I'm always excited to connect with readers like you!

Scan the QR Code Here:

From Nowhere to

Next

MEHMET GONULLU

STARTUP
WISDOM
FROM GLOBAL
FOUNDERS,
BUILDERS, AND
INNOVATORS

Table of Contents

The Outsider's View

I grew up in Lebanon, and though we lived through hard times—there was a civil war back in the '80s and early '90s—it still didn't stop me from being curious about technology. I was fortunate enough to grow up in a home where everyone was encouraged to learn, especially when it came to technology.

This book is for dreamers and doers, whether you're a tech professional itching to start your own venture, an aspiring entrepreneur searching for your purpose, or an ecosystem builder working to create the next innovation hub in your region. If you've ever felt like an outsider looking in on the world of startups, this book is your guide to turning that perspective into your greatest strength.

My father owned an electronics repair shop, and it was here that I first encountered technology. At that time, seeing TV circuits and the insides of electronic devices were *wow* moments for me, sparking my curiosity about innovation.

One time, when I was around six or seven years old, I received an electric shock while playing with circuits. My hands were almost burned, but strangely, that didn't scare me—it only deepened my curiosity. I still remember that moment not as a warning, but as a challenge. It told me that even danger can't stop a curious mind.

Later, when I started attending school, I retained this curiosity about learning more, and I was very passionate about reading every book I could get my hands on about technology. I used to buy the old encyclopedias to learn about physics, science, and everything in between. However, as I grew older and neared college age, I discovered that I enjoy trying new things.

I like entrepreneurship, but at that time, I didn't even know what the word meant. I made some attempts at doing business, but I didn't achieve success. But then I decided one day, *Let me try this. What could I lose?*

It makes me laugh to think about it now, but back then, I didn't know how to create effective advertisements. This was the early days of the internet era, when everything was new and less common than it is today. So, the idea that came to mind was that I would make an advertisement, print it myself, and then stick one in front of every single building. I also stuck them in the elevator of every building, and this is where I started to get customers.

I began learning a great deal about entrepreneurship and starting businesses. Early on, I became more curious about observing those who had succeeded, especially those who had overcome hardships or difficult times similar to mine. I started to notice a few people, especially from Silicon Valley, and I fell in love with the area because that's where Apple devices originated. It was also the birthplace of the Atari, which I started to play and wanted to understand.

I saw the entrepreneurs there, and I began to understand and immerse myself in the world of entrepreneurship and startups. Steve Jobs and others sparked my curiosity and gave me a different perspective on what it takes to be successful.

What I aim to achieve with this book is to provide you with an outsider's perspective on entrepreneurship. For most of my career, I worked as a technician or technologist. I was employed as a consultant and was also involved in a couple of start-ups.

However, I felt that I could add value by sharing what I've learned in my career and professional life, as I started to see a lot of noise and everyone claiming they could provide the magic pill—which, by the way, doesn't exist. This is why I felt that I needed to write a book that could give everyone who reads it a first hope. Second, I could spark something in their minds so they would go and start doing something instead of just sitting on the couch.

I aim to fill the gap in the current conversation about entrepreneurship. I want to make sure that people can think in a different way than they were taught. I want people to challenge the status quo. I want them to think differently because it's possible.

I reached a turning point at the beginning of 2023. I decided to leave a successful career in a very good position where I was working and go out and begin exploring and discovering. I started to wonder about what I could do, and then I decided to start a podcast.

Was it hard to do? Indeed, it was. The hardest part is to take the first step, but once you do, don't think about what happens next; just close your eyes and do it. This was where everything started to take off.

Why? Because I followed an old passion, a gut feeling that had been sitting with me for a long time. I had a purpose, a mission to leave the world a better place than I found it. I also began to think that if these folks could do it, why couldn't I? I wanted to create change. I wanted to spark this entrepreneurial spirit in others. There is a myth that entrepreneurship isn't for everyone, but the truth is that anyone can be an entrepreneur. This is what the podcast started to teach me. I went to school, of course, but the podcast became a university for me.

At first, my format was solo episodes. However, I soon realized that I needed something different, and I started interviewing people. (Of course, maybe the first few weren't the best, but I was learning.)

I tried to see how I could get the best out of my guests, and it ended up that the more you speak to people, the more you learn. Every single episode was a master class for me. Over the last two and a half years, I have accumulated more knowledge and wisdom than I had before starting the podcast. I was surprised by what I learned from my guests: how they got started, how they generated ideas, and how they decided to pursue their endeavors.

I've realized that, sometimes, we might have things in common, but because we don't talk to each other, we're unaware of it. I discovered this when one of my guests told me, "I didn't grow up around tech startups. I grew up seeing people fix things with limited tools, and I said to myself, *This is exactly what I want to do. This is how I can make a difference.*"

Another guest told me, "You don't need access to build something meaningful; you need hunger and the ability to listen harder than everyone else," and this stuck in my head. I realized that I needed to listen, and a podcast is one of the best platforms for that because the host asks questions and then listens. Another guest told me, "We're not trying to do something similar to what they do in Silicon Valley. We're trying to sell solutions to problems the Valley doesn't even see." This also opened my mind because we need to think on a global level.

I wrote this book for any entrepreneur who already has a purpose or is seeking guidance on how to discover their purpose. It's for tech professionals who are dreaming about the next step in their careers and how they can potentially become entrepreneurs, people who are dreaming of starting something big. I'm talking ecosystem builders, those who want to contribute to building something bigger than themselves.

I hope that by reading this book, you will gain some motivation to start building something. I hope that you see the story through my eyes. I hope you gain insight into what I see by listening to my podcast, where I talk to many fellow entrepreneurs.

My goal is to ignite your entrepreneurial spark, giving you the clarity and confidence to start building a business that reflects your purpose. Through my journey—from a curious kid in Lebanon to a podcast host interviewing global founders—I've learned what drives success. This book distills those insights to help you take your first steps, whether it's launching a startup, pivoting your career, or fostering innovation in your community.

CHAPTER 1

Start with Purpose

I always believe that anything we do in life should have a purpose behind it. I'd like to share a story from my own experience that relates to this: starting the podcast.

Hosting a podcast was a long-held dream of mine, and it all began when I was seven. I would record my voice on the tape recorder, acting as if I were a radio broadcaster. Now, at that time, I didn't understand why I was doing this.

However, over time, I began to understand that sharing knowledge and helping people understand what they need to achieve in life, as well as how to pursue a career or start successful companies, is essential. Everything needs to have a purpose, and what I figured out is that the reason I was recording myself when I was young was basically because I wanted to share the knowledge I had.

I started the podcast in January 2023, and my dream became a reality after almost forty years. To provide some context, I initially intended to start it much earlier than that, but due to various life events, I didn't achieve my goal until 2023.

At that time, I didn't see many people sharing knowledge in the way it needed to be done. I felt that people were just doing things for the sake of doing them, for the sake of imitating other people. And when I decided to start recording my podcast, I thought about what things were missing from the masses that I could bring to the forefront with my voice. This is where I was putting my *why*, always front and center.

One time, I wanted to watch the Discovery Channel, but it was only available via satellite. I couldn't afford a dish, so I repurposed the back cover of an old washing machine to act as a satellite dish. I scavenged pieces from an old antenna to hold the LNB in place and found a cheap satellite receiver at a flea market. That's how far I was willing to go just to learn something new. When resources are scarce, determination becomes your most powerful tool.

I have always thought that if we must do something, we first need to believe in it. We also need to make it a mission for ourselves. I always say that—and I've seen it from my experience with a lot of people—sometimes, we think we are passionate about something, but really, we are not.

The best test is to see if you always come back to the same point where, you know, you get dragged to the same topic again and again. For example, the podcast was exactly the same for me. What makes a purpose strong enough to drive long-term action? So we can understand that, really, we are attached to this.

When you're pursuing your purpose, notice what occupies your mind relentlessly. Is there a problem—like improving access to education or streamlining local businesses—that you can't stop brainstorming solutions for, even late at night? Jot down these thoughts daily for a week and then look for patterns. For me, it was the lack of accessible startup knowledge that kept me up, which ultimately led to the creation of my podcast. This exercise helps you pinpoint the mission that drives you.

We often hear about "the hustle," right? Hustle is just you doing something because you need to make a living. You do things, sometimes things you don't like, just to survive. Now, when we talk about a mission, it's something completely different. The mission is the fuel that drives us to achieve something, and we strive for it with a purpose.

People are often confused about the distinction between results and purpose. I always ask people who want to become entrepreneurs: "*Why do you want to become an entrepreneur?*" I got this from Steve Jobs, who said in an interview that this is the question he poses to people who want to become entrepreneurs. Usually, when asked this, people say that they want to become rich, but becoming rich is merely an outcome.

We need to understand our motivation for waking up every day and pursuing something that truly matters to us. Sometimes, you might think, *I feel like I'm getting lost. I'm not entirely sure what my purpose is. I don't know why I'm doing this.* This is fine. It's part of the journey.

In fact, it happened to me at various stages in my life and career. When I was a child, I wanted to become a teacher. And then later, I thought that I would become the guy who drives the trash truck because it looked fun, right? So, I thought my purpose was just to have fun. While growing up, I always thought that I would get a job with a nice title so people would look up to me. However, this wasn't something that truly fulfilled me.

As I mentioned, feeling lost is part of the journey, and there's nothing wrong with you if you do. I think it's part of the life experience, where we need to test ourselves to understand our purpose. Finding your purpose is like going and mining for gold. You get a lot of sand, and you need to filter it out until you find the actual gold. This is not always an easy thing.

You need to have passion, and you need to really get yourself to a place where you put your effort toward finding this purpose. Sometimes, this requires its own journey. It's enough at the beginning to understand that you're looking for your purpose. However, when you find it, it will feel fantastic.

Returning to the podcast, after a while, I insisted on asking one question when I started interviewing people: "Why do you do what you do?" I've heard from many entrepreneurs and successful businesspeople that it took them some time to understand their purpose. They tried, they struggled, and at times, they were lost.

It's perfectly normal to experience this sense of disorientation. But after a while, consistency becomes very important. This is where not losing hope and not losing sight of what you're trying to do are mandatory. This is actually the purpose by itself. So, if you keep trying to do this, your purpose will come to you.

Now, some people ask, "How do I understand that I'm running after a purpose?" The key is that, even if you fall down, you keep coming back and trying again and again.

When I started my podcast, I had zero followers and zero supporters. Actually, I had zero backers. I started with a very cheap microphone and a very loose setup. I decided to just hit the record button because I thought, *What can I lose, right?*

I didn't have much traction initially, but I said, "You know what? I have a mission." I started the podcast because, as I mentioned earlier, my purpose was to share my knowledge and to empower people to do great things. I believed I would have my own startup and achieve success as an entrepreneur.

Because I didn't do this right away, I thought, *Maybe I'm failing.* However, what I discovered is that my strength lies in my ability to effectively communicate with people, extract knowledge from them, and then share it with others. So, I said, "Okay, this is my mission," and I continued on.

I just imagined that the podcast would be a success. I told myself, *Look, if I can even inspire just one person, if I can just touch one single person on this earth, that's fine with me.* And I completed my mission. I inspired others to act on their dreams.

Now, how can people actually succeed once they find their purpose and their mission?. Here, I would like to discuss what I have observed and learned from the people I have met during my career.

I've seen two types of founders and entrepreneurs: those who are obsessed with solving a problem and those who are just looking for external rewards, such as wealth or fame. In my experience, it's the individuals in the first group who tend to succeed. Those in the latter group will chase funding, but when they finally receive the money, they spend it all.

This is where people often confuse something very important—the distinction between mission and ambition. When you are on a mission, you do whatever it takes to succeed. When you are on a mission, you might have sleepless nights, or you might even sleep in your car or office. You're ready mentally and physically to lose everything.

Those with ambition say, "Yeah, I can build a business. If it succeeds, fine." Yeah, it's nice to be a founder. It's nice to be a tech entrepreneur, it's nice to have all these big titles, and it's nice to be mentioned in newspapers and on the internet. However, I've seen people who failed because this is all they wanted. We read these stories nowadays on a daily basis, where we see people who are just ambitious about being a founder versus those who are truly committed to achieving their mission and purpose.

The latter is something I can relate to, having done the same thing myself. I've worked with numerous entrepreneurs throughout my life and career. When people have ambition, they usually burn out very quickly. They feel they are losing it all and give up. People on a mission, however, are obsessed with creating clarity. They are obsessed with success, but they also understand that it will not be easy.

Now, you might be saying, "You're telling us now about this *why* thing. So, how do I find this *why* again?" Well, if you're feeling that you're still searching for your purpose, as I said, you're not alone.

I was in your place years ago. And by the way, it doesn't have anything to do with your age. I've seen people who are fortunate enough to discover their true purpose early in their career, and they've become very successful. I've also seen people who discovered it late, but they've become successful as well. Those who discover it late have an advantage because they've tried other things, and they can share a wealth of knowledge with others. This is essentially me, as I discovered my purpose later in life.

If you're a founder or entrepreneur, or if you're looking for a way to solve a problem, you can alleviate someone's pain today. You just need to put yourself in the situation your customers are facing today. When you do that, you will discover if this is really your purpose. Is this really what you want to do for people? Are you going to take them from point A to point B, or are you just saying, "Hey, I can be your guide, and if you arrive, that's fine. If you don't, sorry. Better luck next time." This is the difference between these two mentalities.

Now, back to discovering your *why*. You should always ask yourself this question: *Why do I want to do what I'm doing?* In answering this, think of the famous concept from Japanese philosophy known as *ikigai*, which means finding something you love, something that you can make money from doing, and something that people would love to have from you.

If you take this first step of discovering how you can find these three common things, it's a very good start. Later, you will experiment. Sometimes, you think you love something, but then you find out that you need to change, and that's completely fine. People in a startup understand that pivoting or changing is a common occurrence, something that can absolutely happen. You don't need to worry about it a lot.

When it comes to your purpose, you need to act as if you are looking for your treasure, and finding a treasure is not something easy. You'll need to do a lot of digging; you'll also have to do a lot of running. You're going to experience some pain during this process, but it's worth it because once you discover your mission and purpose, you become unstoppable. As one of the founders I interviewed told me, "If I stop today, the only regret I have is letting this problem go unsolved."

That's when I knew they were driven by purpose, not ego, because when people are driven by ego, it's tough for them to accept the inevitable defeats that will occur over time. Life has ups and downs. We'll always face challenges, so just keep thinking that you're unbeatable, that you're a superhero.

This doesn't exist in the real world. You become a superhero by being defeated, by getting knocked down multiple times, and then you stand up. This is where you become truly unbeatable. You actually need to be beatable to become unbeatable.

Another guest told me, "My startup didn't begin with a pitch deck; it began with frustration. I was tired of watching people suffer from the same broken process." When these people start to immerse themselves in what people are facing and have a willingness to help them, of course, they like what they do. They enjoy helping people overcome challenges. At the same time, they like the domain and what they are trying to do.

You need to be rational in your thinking, especially if you're just starting your company. You don't go by the book. You always need to decide what you want to offer people, and this is where your mission will become increasingly clear.

Another entrepreneur shared that in the early days, they had no traction, no revenue, just the mission. That's what carried them through the silence. This can happen frequently, and by the way, this is a test to see if you are genuinely able to continue with what you are doing. If you're not mentally prepared to accept that things might go wrong, you may not have someone to listen to you. Even worse, people might also want to kick you out. They won't want to talk to you. They won't want to listen to what you're saying.

If you don't have the mindset of accepting that things can go wrong, there will be negative consequences. This is where having a clear purpose really becomes a cornerstone for everything you do.

So, what methodologies did I use when I began exploring my purpose and mission? Back in 2022, before I started the podcast, I took some time off. I went without any technology—although I'm a tech guy—no mobile phones, no internet, just a notebook and a pen. I began to conduct an audit of my life and tried to recall moments when I felt truly happy doing what I was doing. I wanted to remember these moments because I needed to figure out what I'm passionate about, the things that truly interest me.

After writing tens of points, I narrowed down some categories and realized that they all fell into three main categories. This was where my passion lay. Then my focus shifted to the kinds of problems or shortcomings I had identified that I was eager to address.

Here is where I began to map everything together, searching for something that I love but that people might have a problem with, something that I could solve for them. Finally, I said, "Okay, this is the problem that I like to solve the most," which was essentially the issue I had been living with. I didn't have enough resources to learn about entrepreneurship, startups, and how to be a successful founder, among other things. That was the problem that I fell in love with—and I wanted to fall in love with it because then I could solve it in my own way and offer something to people, which is the podcast and sharing knowledge.

This is why I tell people to fall in love with the problem. Even for founders in technology or any other field, you need to fall in love with the problem. And when I say "fall in love with the problem," that means you need to understand every aspect of this problem. You need to understand why this problem is happening. What are its causes? Your everyday job is to delve deeper and deeper into this problem. This is why we say we love it: you'll be interacting with it a lot.

Once you understand this, ask yourself, *Okay, how can I do it? What can I do to solve this problem?* This is where the passion and drive to put in the effort to solve these problems come together, fueling you to move forward. If you focus on it, you will achieve great success.

The key idea here is that clarity of purpose creates resilience. The more you understand what you're pursuing and why, the more you will accept that you need to keep trying and, if you fail, try again. You eventually end up stronger and get better results. This is where things become significantly better.

CHAPTER 2

The Visionary Mindset

Many times, while watching someone do something, I have wondered, *How were they able to do it? What special skills do they possess to be able to do what they are doing?* I've seen people building, leading, and pitching, and I've thought, *If they can do it, why can't I?* This is something I've asked myself repeatedly.

Since childhood, I have been fascinated by startups, especially those in the late '80s and early '90s in Silicon Valley, the dot-coms. Back then, I said to myself, *Wow, this is fascinating. These guys must have magic. See what they are building. See how they are doing things.*

At some point, I thought, *Okay, this is something I can do myself. Can I repeat what they did?* Now, if I'd wanted to think like all the other kids my age at that time, and even when I was in high school and at university, I would have thought, *I just want to go to school, go home afterward, play a little bit, sleep, and then repeat.*

However, I felt like this was not the life that I wanted. I wanted to stretch. I needed to adopt a different mindset from the people around me so that I could venture into unfamiliar zones. This is why we sometimes refer to it as "leaving your comfort zone." This happened to me several times.

In 2001 or 2002, I became aware of something new: the internet. Not many people were aware of it yet. Interest in the internet was growing rapidly, but there were some issues at the time in establishing connectivity. Few knew how to configure internet-connected devices. Immediately, my entrepreneurial mindset became apparent, as it looked to me like there was an opportunity there. I said, "What can I do to use this situation to start a business?"

When I started discussing the idea with people, they thought I was crazy. They thought it would be difficult and that I would fail miserably. At that time, I had never read about any startups. I'd never had a chance to see a successful entrepreneur in real life. I didn't have any of that. I needed to change my mindset, and as a result, I went all in and started the business.

Initially, it was very successful. Unfortunately, due to the situation in Lebanon, I had to shut it down. That experience was completely fascinating for me because I left my comfort zone. I was a student. I left my studies for almost one year to build the business. Then I went back to school, working part-time until I finished. Ultimately, I had to shut down the business, but it was a success because I left Lebanon.

That experience was a complete mindset shift for me. Since then, I have wanted to keep working with startups. But how? When I left Lebanon,

I was starting from scratch. I came to Dubai with zero in my pocket, absolutely nothing. At that time, in 2005, no one knew what a startup was. What to do? Of course, I started a normal job in IT, where I fixed cables and installed software on PCs.

But I always had this itch for startups. I recall a moment when I saw Steve Jobs' presentation for the iPhone. I said to myself, *Wow, this is the next big thing.*

Again, the entrepreneur in me thought, *How can I benefit from it?* Unfortunately, no one close to me was able to understand what I was saying. But I told everyone I knew, "This smartphone is a revolution. People who can build apps will be wildly successful." Again, no one supported me, but I was able to complete some small tasks that allowed me to build this as a hobby, which gave me a lot of exposure to talk to other startups and people who were doing interesting things.

The magic happened in 2013 when I landed my first job at a startup. That was like the dream of my life. But again, it wasn't easy because I had to leave my comfort zone. Previously, I'd sat in an office, nine to five, where everything was stable and nothing really changed, even from year to year. I spent eight years there, and we had maybe two major changes during that time. It was a very stable environment. However, when you go out and start working with a startup, everything changes.

I have a startup mindset. I like dynamic things. I like to work with changes. We call them "growing pains" in the startup world. These pains were actually painkillers for me. I started to immerse myself in the startups. I wanted to understand why the founders had started the businesses, how they grew them, and how everything was managed. I was very curious about this, and I wanted to understand it as much as possible, to comprehend all the ins and outs.

Working with startups not only changed the way I approached other things, but it also significantly shifted my mindset. Then I started the podcast and, of course, by that time, I had a lot of experience. I'd seen almost everything.

I wanted to treat the podcast as if it were a startup. It became my company, and I decided that we would take a concept and present it to people. If they liked it, that would be fine, but we started thinking about how we could enhance it and make it better.

The vision here was to do something to the maximum, as people would expect it to be. This was how I started the podcast. Of course, I had to do a lot of pivoting. I started solo, but then I began conducting interviews. I discovered that this approach is the best for two reasons: first, it adds value to the audience, and second, it also benefits me.

After two and a half years, I still ask myself, *How can I make this podcast better? How can I take it to the next level? What's the next step to take to expand this podcast's global reach?* Of course, the purpose is very important, but it's just as important to communicate that vision to other people so they can understand what you are trying to do. This is the kind of mindset that it really takes to succeed.

As an entrepreneur, the first thing you need to have is curiosity. Keep asking questions. If someone tells you, "Hey, this is a new calculator," don't just say, "Yeah, okay, fine." You should be asking questions.

The first question you should ask is, "Where was this calculator manufactured?" followed by, "Why does it have this number of buttons?" If you don't ask these questions, that means you are not ready to be an entrepreneur and a founder because you need to question every single thing.

Don't get me wrong. It's not enough to ask for the sake of asking. You need to do this because you want to ensure that what you're trying to do aligns with your purpose. This is where curiosity comes. You need to ask a lot of questions. You need to ensure, every time, that whatever is done is done the right way.

This goes back to having the love to solve a problem or a pain, so you need to understand why you want to enhance this. What's the problem people are seeing today, or what pain are they experiencing? Are they waiting too long to fulfill something? Are they paying a lot of money to get something? We always need to have an urge to alleviate the pain. If you see something, ask a question like: "How long does it take?" Then, when you find out that the answer is ten minutes. ask, "Can it be done in three?" You always need to do this.

I would like to add one very important thing. If you ask why something is done a certain way, and someone tells you that it's because that's the way other people do it, you should ask more questions. You should not accept what they tell you. Never accept the status quo—always challenge it.

This is the kind of mindset that enables you to have a clear vision and achieve your goals. But at the same time, you also need to be calm. So, you need to understand that sometimes you can feel angry or frustrated about something that's happening, which is perfectly normal. We are all human, so we might sometimes feel like we are under pressure.

However, you need to stay calm for your vision to stay clear. Sometimes, what happens with founders and entrepreneurs is that they receive different feedback from the right, left, and center. Some people say, "Hey, you should do this…" Others say, "You should do that…" You need to remain calm under pressure and maintain clarity so that you don't get pulled in multiple directions at once.

You should also stay optimistic, and don't mess it up by being stubborn. Tell yourself, *This will succeed,* especially if everyone's telling you, "No, this cannot be done." Now, if you've tested it yourself many times and see that it's not feasible, you need to know when to stop and pivot a bit, because there's a very thin line between being practical and being stubborn.

Again, it's nothing about your ego. It's just accepting the facts. However, I always say that, if possible, you should have the proof that we need to make the change. But again, stay curious and ask a lot of questions.

Now, how do you define this vision? Some people say you should write down ideas, but that's not enough. Also, being visionary is not just about saying something like, "Okay, I'm dreaming of a car that can fly." Yeah, it's nice to think about it. But this is just an idea, which is just a thought on paper.

What it really takes to be visionary is to think about how you're going to use this idea. Start to think about what you're going to do day and night with all the challenges that you might face to reach that idea. This is what I call the vision: you need to imagine a world and envision yourself manifesting that world in the future. At the same time, imagine yourself completing the journey to get there.

So, can someone build something meaningful if they weren't born with wealth or talent? Yes, because the idea that people are born with the necessary skills or that only people with silver spoons in their mouths can become successful is a myth.

I've spoken to many people who come from very humble backgrounds. They had very tough childhoods, and they weren't special in school or anything, but because they had a vision, because they had curiosity and challenged the status quo, they were able to achieve their goals.

It's a long and challenging journey. Just as you have to go to the gym to build muscles, you have to work to build a vision. It doesn't happen overnight. You can't just do it with one click. That's not possible. But can expose yourself to new ideas. You can read more books. You can connect with successful individuals in the same field as you. You also need to take some time for yourself and switch off. You need to have the time to reflect on what's happening.

Sometimes, you need to have the courage to take bold actions. You don't need to ask permission from others to do it, but you need to take action, and sometimes, you need to surround yourself with people who can help you achieve this. You also need to stay away from the naysayers, because they will tell you that it's not doable, not possible, and not to waste your time.

However, there's one point I want to emphasize here, which is the connection between burnout and the ego. I talked about this in the previous chapter because you need to understand that this mindset doesn't have to make you blind as well.

So, when I say you have to manifest the future, you need to put all your attention and focus on that. Now, you don't need to disconnect yourself completely from reality to do this. It also doesn't mean that you just have a dream and then walk into the fire. That is not what I'm asking you to do. What you need to do is maintain a balance. Accept that, sometimes, it's okay to be wrong and make adjustments.

I've seen it many times. My podcast guests have often shared with me that a vision is just a decision to act on a pattern before others recognize it. It looks risky from the outside, but it looks obvious from the inside. That really resonated with me. Acting on the patterns is very important because, once we identify what we are seeing, we can then take the next step, even if it looks risky from the outside.

One founder told me that, despite everyone saying that his idea was crazy, he couldn't stop thinking about it. In other words, for him, it wasn't just a vision; it was a calling. I have heard this from many of my guests: "The vision is that you always keep dreaming about it. How are you going to get there?"

Another guest explained to me that real visionaries aren't loud. In fact, they spend more time listening than talking. I can't stress this enough. People often think that if you have a vision, you need to constantly share it with everyone, which is true, but you also need to maintain a feedback loop. This is where you can really avoid burnout. You can also avoid going in the wrong direction while thinking that you are heading the right way.

As you can see, building a visionary mindset is crucial for success. One thing that works for me, especially when I begin each podcast, is to think about where I want to take it, what I want to achieve with this podcast, and what I want people to remember about it, perhaps even decades later. Then I ask myself how I can do that. This exercise will help you find the path to developing the right mindset. And remember, the vision will only grow as far as your mindset allows.

CHAPTER 3

Take the Leap and Keep Learning

Many times, I have had to stop what I was doing to try something new. The first time, as I explained in the previous chapter, I had to step out of my studies for a while to build my first business. The second time I did it was when I left a very comfortable job to work for startups. The third time I did it was when I started the podcast. And then, one day, not long ago, I found myself speaking in public to a large audience.

Every single one of these changes was a big leap for me, and one of the things that allowed me to make them was that I didn't overthink them. Every single one of these moments was scary, but I tried to overcome this by saying, "Okay, what will happen if I don't do it? Do I want to keep doing what I'm doing today?" The answer, always, was to go for it.

The biggest leap I can remember taking is when I found myself on stage in front of more than five hundred people. I had never done a public speaking event before and was quite nervous. But then I thought, *Okay, what's the worst that can happen? It's not like they're going to throw water bottles or tomatoes at me. What can it really cost me? In fact, it will cost me more if I don't do it.*

What happened next is history. I managed to take a step back and force my brain to consider the consequences of *not* doing it—and how I might regret not trying in the future. Turns out, watching inspiring commencement speeches helped, especially those from people I admired—Steve Jobs in particular. The talk didn't just go well; after I finished, I was overwhelmed by congratulations from my colleagues and audience members, many of whom came up to me with questions.

I've hit rock bottom multiple times. I've lost jobs, and I've lost money. In 2017, I was financially broken—literally counting coins—but something inside me, the voice of the entrepreneur, kept saying, *You can start again.* That mindset kept me going. Eventually, I got an opportunity to join a startup I had admired for years: Rubrik. That moment was a reminder that belief in yourself doesn't erase hardship. However, it gives you the courage to climb out of it.

This mindset has given me the confidence to take on challenges. Ultimately, life is about taking the leap. It's always taking action today so we can reach what we want. As of this writing, I have hosted over five hundred podcast episodes. I've advised startups and funds on multiple continents, and I own my story.

If I hadn't started my own business right after college, I wouldn't be doing all this today. So, it wasn't just about getting out of my comfort zone; it was about finding clarity—not only with respect to what I wanted to achieve, but also in terms of where I wanted to end up.

Now, it's not easy. The road will be extremely challenging. Sometimes, it feels like we're climbing a mountain, but we don't know what's on the other side. Are we going to reach the nice beach with the friendly dog, a place to rest and enjoy ourselves before embarking on the next journey? Or are we going to find a desert? If we dwell on this, we might never have the courage to keep climbing.

Every time I decided to do something, it was, of course, never easy. I doubted myself. I felt that maybe people would laugh at me and mock me for what I was doing, but I always thought positively about the results that would come.

I asked myself, *What could go wrong? What's the worst thing that can happen? What will happen if I don't try?* I always try to phrase the question in such a way that it seems easier to do it than not to do it. This is where taking the leap is crucial.

Starting a company, especially in the tech sector, is not an easy decision to make. Many founders I have spoken with came from very decent jobs. They were working with big tech companies, receiving nice paychecks.

If they hadn't had the mentality of taking the leap, and understood that staying with the comfort they had would mean not learning anything new, they would never have started their companies. This is the mindset I've observed working again and again: accepting that ambiguity can be a positive thing, especially when you're an entrepreneur. Having this uncertainty is a significant strength, as it's better to be uncertain than to feel like you're not advancing in your career.

So, keep learning. Keep trying to do the next thing. You might ask, "But how can I do this? I've been doing this for years. Can I change now?" Age can make things a little difficult, but it's still doable because all it requires is a change in mindset. You just need to believe that the only way you can lose is if you don't do it.

I learned this from my podcast guests. They all had ideas, but what they really shared was the itch to implement them. They felt that if they didn't do it, someone else would, and they would lose the chance to be the leaders of the domain in which they were trying to create something new. This helped them understand that they needed to continue learning and taking the leap.

It's important to understand that this is not something that happens overnight. It's about testing something, failing, and learning from the experience. I call this the "test-and-learn" mindset. If you say, "I've got to leave my comfort zone and take the leap, but let me do the proper planning first," you are taking the first step to failure because, if you plan too much, you are actually planning to fail.

I'm not saying don't plan. I'm not saying to just take blind risks. What I'm trying to say here is that you need to take small steps daily, learn from what works and what doesn't, and then adjust accordingly.

But if you just make a big plan and start to execute, what will happen—and it happened to me many times—is that at the first hiccup you face, you will think that the whole plan is not working. Then you'll waste your time putting together another big plan, and this process will repeat itself again and again. This is why, using a startup or agile mentality, you need to approach things step by step, allowing yourself to adapt, change, and shift based on the outcomes you observe. You cannot do everything in one step.

Building a brand takes patience and iteration, like crafting a startup itself. Start by sharing one authentic story—perhaps a LinkedIn post about why you launched your venture or a customer testimonial video. Test its impact: did it resonate with your audience? Adjust based on feedback and then share another. My podcast grew by posting raw, honest clips about my guests' struggles, which built trust over time. Consistent, small steps create a lasting brand.

You also need to understand that you must rest and settle down sometimes if things are not working fine. Try to identify what made you uncomfortable and assess how that discomfort affected you. Then, with time, you can start to see what that discomfort is teaching you.

Genuinely ask yourself, *What is really annoying me? Why am I not into doing this?* Then keep asking yourself these questions until you find the answers. Then you will discover that there is a way out. The most important thing is being ready to feel discomfort because taking a leap is not easy.

It's like living in a mansion today and, tomorrow, going to live in a tent. It can't happen all at once. You need to prepare yourself over time, and the way to do this is to shift the way you think. It's essential to understand that experiencing moments of uncertainty is normal. Uncertainty is not based on real danger. It's based on the possibility of danger, and if you keep overthinking things, you will never move.

Many people tell themselves, "I'm going to do this tomorrow," and they keep doubting: "Oh, what if this happened? What if this came up?" They keep themselves in uncertainty, and this is the number one reason why people don't start at all. I've seen founders and entrepreneurs who, due to this uncertainty, become paralyzed, and their businesses fail because they weren't prepared to understand that uncertainty isn't a danger; it's a possibility.

Now, of course, this doesn't mean that we just throw ourselves from the top of the cliff. We need to take calculated risks, but there's an illusion here between stability and risk. With all the noise surrounding us, we are programmed to understand that certain jobs and industries are considered the safest. We need to truly unfilter reality and see it with the naked eye to understand if this is really an illusion or not. We should say, "Yeah, I might have a stable job and income, but at what cost? What am I risking by staying here?" At the same time, if you decide to step out, what are you losing and what are your gains?

You need to understand that you must always calculate your risks. You need to have control over the outcome levels, but not certainty. You need to ask, "If I do this, what will happen? If I do this other thing, what will happen?" It is very common to feel uncertain, especially if you are a first-time entrepreneur or founder. However, time will help you learn to handle it, and the best approach is to tackle things in phases rather than risking it all at once.

Some people advise—especially for those who are already working, have established careers, and are willing to become entrepreneurs— that you start the business as a side hustle, using it as a form of preparation before taking the leap to full-fledged business owner.

Not everyone can just jump over the fire. Sometimes, you just need to stay next to the fire, get accustomed to the heat, and then take the leap. This is what I call calculated risk and having control over the outcome levels.

However, there is a trap that people sometimes fall into: the idea that we've seen it all, we don't need to do anything, and we are fine. So, the common excuse is, "Why do I need to do this? Why do I need to learn something new? Why do I need to take this leap? Why do I need to start this?" The majority of the time, this happens because we've become tied to the life we're living, and we're not willing to go out and pursue our purpose, our mission.

Sometimes this is caused by people around you who convince you that you don't need to learn. However, in today's fast-paced world, especially with the advent of AI, no one can claim to know it all. No one can claim that they don't need to learn something new. This is something very common that I see.

The second trap I see people falling into is not being empathic. Empathy is crucial, and when you take a leap, you need to do so with empathy. You need to put your soul into it. You need to decide that the leap you are taking has a purpose; it will lead to something that you want to achieve. You need to feel fully committed and lean in to be successful in taking this leap.

Sometimes, you don't take the leap because you're surrounded by the wrong people or the wrong network. The best approach I've seen working here is to have someone who can act as a critic for you, someone who will keep you accountable. This is where, the majority of the time, people mix (especially in entrepreneurship) the team around them with friends.

You don't need friends here. You don't need people to applaud you; you need someone to keep you accountable. You need someone who will ask you the hard questions: "Have you done the work necessary to take the leap today? Have you done what you promised you would do to be in a better position today?"

In a world where everything is moving fast, disruption is constant; therefore, you must continually learn. If you don't, in a couple of years, you will be outdated. Someone else will come and take your dream from you and make it a reality. So, the only way for you to do it is to keep learning. Nothing is static anymore, and education is not the same as it was years ago. We must remain prepared for disruptions.

Of course, the last twenty years have shown us that things can change overnight. We've seen how Netflix destroyed Blockbuster and how the iPhone put Nokia and BlackBerry out of business, as well as numerous other instances where a new company displaced one that didn't want to take the leap. We've seen it again and again.

Don't be that guy who is stubborn and not willing to learn because he thinks that he's got it all. You should always maintain a mindset of continuous learning. But you might say, "How do I learn? Do I have to go to school? Do I have to go take courses?" Not necessarily.

There are plenty of ways to do it. If you're willing to learn, you can find resources everywhere. To stay ahead as an entrepreneur, seek knowledge strategically. Start with one resource that aligns with your goals—for example, read *The Lean Startup* by Eric Ries for practical startup strategies or listen to the *How I Built This* podcast for founder stories. Dedicate fifteen minutes daily to learning, perhaps during your commute or before bed. I carved out time to read startup blogs while working full time in Dubai, which fueled my podcast ideas. Small, consistent efforts keep you competitive in a fast-moving world.

And don't tell me you don't have time. Technology today provides access to books with thousands of pages, summarized in a way that is concise enough to motivate you and provide a solid foundation for learning. So, you don't have to wait to learn everything.

I encourage people to continue learning, reading, and engaging with others. Here's how you can do this continually. It worked for me, and it was the best decision that I ever made when I took the leap to start the podcast. In every single interview I do, it's not just about asking questions and having nice conversations with my guests. It's about me learning from them. Each podcast episode is a masterclass from someone exceptional in technology, marketing, entrepreneurship, public relations, or any other field.

As a result, the podcast became a valuable source of learning for me, as I spoke with people and asked them questions. Asking questions is very important. Be curious. Don't accept the status quo.

One of my guests left a stable corporate job to launch a business in a market they had never worked in before. They said, "I didn't feel ready. I just felt like I was done waiting." This is really stuck in my head because this founder could have waited a lot longer before starting what they wanted to do, but there was an itch inside to go and solve this problem. So, they took the leap, left their corporate job, and nailed it.

Another founder shared that every time he took a leap, he felt unqualified. However, that discomfort is always part of the free learning experience. Trying something new opens the mind. It lets you feel like a child again.

One of the CTOs I interviewed told me, "I don't hire for perfect skills. I hire relentless learners. The future belongs to them." This is so true. Today, the most successful people in the marketplace, whether in startups or corporations, are those who are eager to learn new concepts, not those who merely walk past books.

You might say, "How can I take the leap?" My advice here is to choose one skill that you need to develop and have wanted to develop for a long time. Start very small. Find a book about it. Find a podcast about it. Find a documentary about it, and you don't have to do everything in one step. There are numerous books, particularly self-help books, that suggest taking baby steps. Through compounding, you will reach your goal.

So, start small, pick that one skill, master it, and then share it after one month, one year, or five years. The important thing is to start today, this very day, because if you don't, your dreams will die, and you will never achieve success as an entrepreneur. You need to talk, take bold actions, and fuel yourself for this next evolution.

CHAPTER 4

Build Your Own Blueprint

I'm sure every one of you, at some stage, has heard someone say, "Copy this playbook, and you will succeed."

Have you ever blindly followed someone else's plans and regretted it? Actually, I did. When I was younger, I would often see advertisements on TV, and then on the internet as it became more widespread, claiming to hold the key to success. And still, we see this today, where people mention that if you simply copy what they've done, you will succeed.

Of course, I learned by trying this multiple times until I finally understood that if someone is doing this, though it might have worked for them, it won't necessarily work for me. When it comes to starting specialty businesses in the tech industry, I've seen people who fall into this trap. The reason for this, I believe, is human nature. We like to take shortcuts.

We like it, and there is nothing wrong with that. It's very normal because we are always trying to either save time or conserve the energy we are supposed to expend. And when it comes to starting businesses— we see it in tech a lot of times—people start businesses because they've seen other people doing it successfully, and they think they can imitate their efforts. They start to copy, and they become what we call "copycats." By the way, copycats will always exist.

Some might argue that there's nothing wrong with a copycat if they can do the job better, which is a valid point. However, the issue here is that people who promote this concept often do so in the wrong way. They encourage people, especially younger entrepreneurs, to take shortcuts just to prove that they don't need to put in the effort. The result is that the business isn't something that they felt they needed to do. It isn't their main purpose.

As we discussed in the first chapter, they didn't ask themselves why they were starting this business. After a while, they get lost. I've seen this repeatedly. And, of course, many of my podcast guests have confirmed this as well.

Let's pause for a minute and think about the "one size fits all" myth. Let's take, for example, one of the most successful startups of all time: Facebook. If anyone could imitate what Facebook has done, then why don't we have thousands, if not millions, of people who have built Facebooks and succeeded? And by the way, at one point, it was common to see people say, "Hey, I can teach you how to create a clone of Facebook in just two days so you can start your own social media company."

When the gig economy began to take off and websites like Fiverr and Upwork gained mainstream popularity, everyone wanted to offer the same services by simply copying and pasting. And yeah, you didn't need to do anything. However, the reality is that the unicorns didn't follow a single path.

People who are first movers, especially those who are the first to enter a new market, often face significant challenges. Of course, we can learn from their mistakes. We can learn from the things that went wrong, and I'm not saying that we shouldn't create new businesses that can compete in that space, but there are some conditions.

First, can we offer what they do in an easier way? If they offer something that requires a lot of time today, can we offer it to people in a shorter time? Can we do it more cost-effectively? Actually, if we can challenge them when they become the status quo, yes. Now we can claim that we are a startup challenging an established business by offering our own unique edge. We cannot just copy. And this doesn't apply just to ideas. It applies to every step we need to take to build a successful business.

I've seen the concept of "one size fits all" applied not only to generating ideas and starting a business, but also to the execution. As a result, when people try to launch a business, they often fail to execute because they believe that if they copy the execution plans of others, they will succeed as well.

There isn't a step-by-step guide to building a business. You're going to try, fail, and try again. Do this, and you'll start to see traction, what we call the "startup space," a product-market fit. To achieve a good product-market fit, you need to time your business launch effectively, and you must also consider the market's maturity to effectively receive your business and idea.

We've seen many times where some concept failed because the timing was wrong. For example, PDAs, or portable devices that assist people in their day-to-day work tasks, initially failed but ultimately succeeded with the introduction of iPhones and later iPads by Apple. The first time wasn't the right time.

Additionally, the market may sometimes reject ideas. We've seen this again and again. We saw how Facebook became the primary social media platform, but sites like Friendster and other social media websites failed because the market wasn't mature enough for them.

I have a theory, and it says that we live in a three-dimensional world. Everyone talks about three dimensions as a spatial system, but the three dimensions I am referring to are place, time, and personality. These three things are what really shape your path to success.

Once you understand these three dimensions, you will start to have an edge in building your own blueprint. Geography, or location, is one factor because if you were born in, let's say, India, you may not have the same resources as someone born in the U.S. Or if you were born in Latin America, it's not the same as being born in Japan. So, geography affects your personality, which is the third dimension.

Now, the time you were born, your age, and what you have seen also affect things. Why am I mentioning this? Because if someone is successful, it's often because they were in the right place at the right time.

An accumulation of cultural and educational factors, day-to-day interactions with people, and other experiences shape personality. This is where you have an edge, but if you try to apply the same formula to different dimensions, it will fail to yield the same results. Even in physics, you cannot apply the same formula in all locations because gravity changes, and everything else is affected by gravity, including mass and velocity. Think about it.

Now, that doesn't mean you are unlucky because you were born in a place that is not as developed as another. Actually, this might give you an edge in terms of your personality, and it might also give you an edge in terms of time.

Here are a few examples:

Jumia, often called the "Amazon of Africa," didn't just replicate a model—it reimagined e-commerce for a fragmented, low-trust market by introducing pay-on-delivery, its own logistics network, and digital literacy efforts.

Nubank, dubbed the "Revolut of Latin America," responded to Brazil's broken banking system with a no-fee, mobile-first experience, winning massive adoption where incumbents had failed to modernize.

Careem, known as the "Uber of the Middle East," succeeded by adapting ride-hailing to regional norms, offering cash payments, call center booking, and culturally sensitive options long before global players understood the local context.

These weren't clones—they were smart, localized bets, shaped by timing, geography, and cultural understanding.

Again, what works in the U.S. doesn't necessarily work in Europe. And what works in Europe doesn't necessarily work in Japan. And what works in Japan might not work in Australia. Why? The answer encompasses cultural nuances, language, and local network connections. It had to do with the way people do business.

We need to keep all of this in mind when we decide to build our own venture. It's very important to understand this combination of the three dimensions: place, time, and personality. Otherwise, simply copying something may not always be effective. It might work once, but I assure you, with time, it will fail.

Previously, I discussed spotting signals. So, what does it mean to spot a signal? What it means is the ability—and you will develop this with time and experience—to recognize patterns. Pattern recognition is the ability to identify what people want to buy from you, whether you are selling to mass consumers or businesses, and to anticipate the next thing they are ready to purchase. This requires a lot of work. Again, you cannot simply replicate something blindly.

As someone I admire a lot, Professor Steve Blank of Stanford University, says, "You need to step out of the building. You cannot just read manuscripts. You cannot just read guides. You cannot just read step-by-step documents and expect results." And as Einstein is purported to have said, "Insanity is doing the same thing again and again and expecting different results."

So, you need to be able to step out and do your own thing. Without doing that, simply copying others without truly understanding why you're doing it and building your own blueprint, it won't work. I've seen this on the podcast with my guests.

One founder told me he was based in the MENA region (Middle East, North Africa). He said, "We copied what worked from a unicorn in the U.S., and we nearly went bankrupt." Then he added, "After that experience, we only built for our context and our region. Then things started to click."

Another guest shared how pattern recognition isn't about copying. It's understanding why it worked and when to adapt it to your reality. And yet another founder told me there's no one-size-fits-all. You build the blueprint while you walk the path. You learn by doing it.

My advice, if you're already starting or thinking about starting your next venture and want to be successful, is to read a lot of books and review all the success stories. Do this for one single reason: to get inspiration. Don't put in your mind that you are going to be successful because you're going to copy exactly what they have done. You need to put your own strategies in place.

Believe me, once you immerse yourself in this experience, you will be successful. I like to say, "Inspiration is a fuel. It's not your GPS." Just take it as your daily food, and then you will be able to thrive and survive even in tough times.

CHAPTER 5

Build Your Story,
Build Your Brand

In today's world, with so much noise around us, all businesses, founders, and entrepreneurs need to focus on branding. And when I say branding, I don't mean branding in the traditional way of just, you know, creating a logo and having colors and taglines.

Things are changing, and I discovered this through my podcast. People nowadays look at more than just what you are offering, whether it's a product, service, or even entertainment. They want to be personally and emotionally connected to what you are offering, and you can't do this without a story.

The story is how you convey your purpose, which we discussed in Chapter One. You bring your vision and all the things you've done to build this business, and you present it to the audience, who are likely your future customers. So, how did I discover this? As I mentioned earlier, I discovered this through my passion for the podcast. I wanted to build it, and I wanted to be transparent with my audience. So, I wanted to choose a name that reflected the purpose I was after. This is why I chose to call it *The CTO Show with Mehmet.*

CTO is a technical term that stands for chief technology officer, a role in companies, whether small or large, whose main function is to translate technical terms into business-understandable language. The CTO serves as the link between technology and business, and I felt that I needed to present this.

My audience is a mix of two worlds: technology and business. Having experience in these areas allows me to feel that I'm capturing the attention of both groups.

I deal with my podcast as though it's a startup, so I wanted to build it in the same way startups are being built today. I want people to remember the podcast when they see me and, when they see the podcast, to remember me.

This is something, honestly, that I have spent some time on. I could have just asked ChatGPT (which was out by this time), "Hey, I'm thinking of doing this podcast concept. Give me some names and suggestions." I didn't do that.

I really sat down and spent half a day just imagining how people would react when they saw me or the podcast, and what they would relate to. Finally, I settled on three key terms: "insights, ideas, and innovation." I wanted to provide people with insights about technology. I wanted to inspire them to generate new ideas and then go out and start innovating, achieving success in whatever they did, and not necessarily as founders. Maybe they would become successful leaders. Perhaps they would become successful tech entrepreneurs and leaders. This is what I wanted to focus on when I decided to start my brand.

Now, here's what personal branding is not. Some people confuse personal branding with simply showing up every day without a clear purpose. When building your business brand, remember to always connect the personal perspective behind your actions to the business you are running, the startup you are building.

What makes a founder's brand magnetic? First of all, keep yourself authentic. Don't force yourself to do things that you are not fully convinced you have to do. You need to ensure that you are conveying an emotional connection between you and your audience.

Put yourself in other people's place and think, *Okay, if someone sees this post on LinkedIn, or if someone watches or listens to this podcast that I have recorded, what kind of impression would they have about me?* If you just like to speak about hype and something not relatable, or if you show empathy but don't communicate why you're doing what you're doing, people will not take you seriously.

Here is where you need to work on your storytelling a lot. If you want to master storytelling, the first thing I advise you to do—and there are numerous resources available on the internet for this—is to watch successful founders speaking, whether to their customers, to graduates at commencement, or even to their employees in internal meetings.

Storytelling is an art, but it can be learned. It takes a lot of time to be able to leave your comfort zone and be authentic. Let's be honest with ourselves. All of us, and this is human nature, want to show ourselves at our best all the time. However, with storytelling, sometimes, you need to show your vulnerabilities. You need to speak the truth as it is and without filters. Why? Because people will relate to you when you do. When they relate to you, they will trust you, and when they trust you, they will trust what you are building.

Being authentic is crucial when building your brand, and you achieve this by sharing stories. It doesn't always have to be personal stories. You don't need to share everything. However, you need to focus on the things that can truly resonate with your audience. They will appreciate this.

The one person I know who used to do this perfectly was Steve Jobs. If you watch his famous commencement speech at Stanford University, you will understand what he meant when he talked about his life. He divided the speech into three parts, and in each part, he talked about his personal story. He constantly related what he was saying to Apple, and at the same time, he offered advice to the graduates.

This is the best thing you can ever watch if you want to see what I mean by authentic storytelling. And of course, he mastered it. Throughout all the Apple announcements, especially during his second phase as Apple CEO, we saw how he excelled in this area.

Every CEO I've had the chance to know personally or watch from afar has mastered the art of storytelling. Like them, you need to immerse yourself in people's pain, especially if you're selling a product or service. You need to show authentically why you're building your business.

Eventually, you will need to scale up your approach. In today's world, people often follow communities. People follow those who care about them.

The most successful startups, including those I work directly with, especially in the tech sector, are those that successfully build communities. So, what do I mean by this? To put it plainly, you need to have people who can sell when you are not there. In sales language, we refer to them as "champions."

To have a lot of champions, you need to build a community for them so they can interact and share stories among themselves. When, as the founder or leader, you authentically care about the same objective that these people want to achieve, they will become your ambassadors. They become your sales force when you're not there.

I have had numerous discussions like this with my guests. One founder mentioned that their conversion rate didn't improve after redesigning their website. They kept trying, changing the colors and logos. Things only improved when they rewrote their story. People began to relate to them better.

Another guest told me that if your story doesn't resonate with the right people, that means you don't have a brand, you have noise. This happens a lot. Going back to the previous chapter, if you just follow the ready-made cheat sheets and step-by-step guides, you will have noise, not a brand.

Another guest shared this quote with me: "I stopped pretending to be polished. That's when people actually started to trust me." He then mentioned how he had always been trying, especially on social media, to portray himself as perfect, that the team was perfect, and that everything was going fine. However, things were not going well with them because they actually had problems. When they started to be more authentic and he began to share his failures, people started to trust him.

Now, what advice can I offer to help you build your story and brand? First, go back and start with your purpose. Once you have your purpose, imagine that people are watching you. They might be your customers. They might be your business partners. Try to think about this purpose from their point of view.

Is this something that they would care about? If yes, why do they care about it? The best thing you can do is keep asking questions until you are convinced that this purpose has a story behind it. Once you discover that story, you will be unstoppable because you will have developed empathy and authenticity.

I did this with my podcast. It was the best strategy ever. Not only did people start to see me and get to know me, but, more importantly, they also started to trust me. I know that when I recommend the founders or business partners I work with, my audience trusts me and knows that I will not suggest something that is not suitable for them.

One founder I spoke with built a successful business around virtual events. However, as digital fatigue increased, they noticed that engagement was dropping. Instead of pushing harder into digital, they listened. They recognized a deeper need: audiences want to feel something tangible.

So, they pivoted. They began designing branded physical experiences— carefully curated boxes delivered to customers, each item chosen not only for its utility, but also to tell a story. It wasn't about swag. It was about story. This shift transformed their offering from an event logistics service into an emotional, memorable brand-building tool.

The breakthrough came when clients realized these physical touchpoints created stronger bonds than any email or video ever could. Engagement increased, referrals grew, and what started as a tactical change evolved into a strategic edge. This wasn't just a pivot in format—it was a pivot in how they told their story.

This is how you build your brand and strategy. Avoid falling into the trap of merely collecting impressions and likes.

CHAPTER 6

Geography, Culture, and the Connector Effect

One thing I want to share with you is how, sometimes, you can change someone's story by just making a connection. When I started the podcast, I never thought I would be able to do it, but it was something I had always dreamed about.

As the host of a podcast, I have the opportunity to speak with many people, my guests. And, of course, I get the chance to talk to many of the people who are connected because they've heard about the podcast, watched it somewhere, or some people might have recommended it to them to check it out.

I started the podcast in 2023, and near the end of that year, I interviewed one guest who happened to be in San Francisco, an ex-founder and angel investor. A few months later, at the beginning of 2024, someone reached out to me who wasn't a guest; he had come to show me what he was building.

After speaking with him, I felt that there would be a synergy between him and the guest. I knew that both of them were living in the Bay Area, so I said, "Hey, I think I have to introduce you to someone I know. He was a guest on the podcast." Of course, I asked for both people's permission before making the introductions.

What happened was magic. These two people were just two squares away from each other, but they had never met. I'm in Dubai, while they both live in Silicon Valley, but I was able to connect them. This touched me deeply, and I began to understand the power of connecting people and the importance of understanding different markets.

I began to believe that this is also one of the podcast's missions. I have repeated this process multiple times with different people, but the other times, they were located in different geographical areas. This is how I started to see the power of being a connector.

Being a great connector means bringing people together without expecting anything in return. Believe it or not, if good things happen, you will be compensated in one way or another. This was something that opened my eyes to a deeper understanding of geography and culture and how, as a connector, I can play a role in bringing people together.

One thing I have done frequently in my career is work with numerous startups. Some of them were based in the U.S. and Europe, and they were expanding into new markets, such as the Middle East and North Africa, collectively referred to as the MENA market. I soon learned that just because a business was successful in the place where it started, this isn't always the case when it shifts to a different geographical area.

The point is that we needed to do something different, and this was not related to technology. It was not related to branding. It was not related to marketing. It turned out that this was related to understanding how businesses in different geographies decide to make purchases.

It was the way they procured software, let's say. It was the difference in how they preferred to be reached. Did they like a cold outreach? Did they not like it? The answer affected how we presented the messaging to them.

I learned a great deal here, which I would like to share with you. The first thing to note is that what works in the U.S. won't necessarily work in Europe, and what works in Europe may not work in Singapore. The reason for this is that cultural differences play a big role. You need to understand that each geographical area has its own unique culture. And even within the same country, you sometimes encounter different cultures and varying business practices among people.

I was fortunate enough to work with multinational companies that were expanding into various regions. This has given me an edge in learning how to take the original message and adapt it into a local form that people will accept.

Here's an example to illustrate this point. If you're trying to sell someone something, it's very normal to discuss their current situation and why, for instance, the technology they're using is outdated or inadequate, how it's outdated, and why they should go with a new technology, whether it's faster, cheaper, or maybe more secure.

In some areas, doing this in a straightforward manner doesn't work because people may feel that they are being confronted. They feel that you are trying to tell them that they have made wrong decisions in the past, and now you're trying to outsmart them by claiming you have a better solution.

Don't make this mistake. This is where you really need to spend some time, especially when you move from one geographic area to another. You need to see what works in this area, rather than focusing on what worked well in the place where you started.

People often mistakenly assume that this only applies when moving from the West to the East, but I've seen individuals and founders make this mistake when they try to go from the East to the West and need to adjust their approach to presenting themselves to customs. This is the primary reason why some founders fail when attempting to scale globally. Scaling in different regions doesn't necessarily work the same way, and it often doesn't happen at the same speed.

Additionally, one of the common mistakes founders make is assuming that if they simply invest more money in the business and hire salespeople, they will scale in the same way they did in their original location. This is not always the case, as you need to understand that some markets are slower than others. You need to understand that not all messages are accepted in the same way everywhere you go.

From day one, you also need to decide that you are going to build a business you believe in and that you truly believe can one day become a global brand, so you need to do your research. You need to ask, does your logo fit all cultures? Will it elicit a negative reaction from any group or any nationality? You need to examine your slogans. You need to see all your marketing materials. You need to understand that when shifting from one geographic area to another, you don't need to reinvent everything from scratch. I've seen people fail because of this, and this is where I was able to contribute to many startups by talking to the founders and helping them understand these issues.

Now, even if you are a founder or entrepreneur, it's beneficial to put yourself in a connector role within your team. When you immerse yourself in the cultures of other geographies, you should go back home and share with them all the things you saw there so that you can build successful messaging—and not only with technology, because technology is the same across all borders.

What matters is how you communicate with people, how you engage with them, and how you serve them after they've purchased from you. This is very important. I recall many of my guests discussing this topic, but one guest shared, "Our tech was ready to scale. However, our message failed in every new market until we stopped assuming that every buyer thinks the same way."

This really resonated with me because I've experienced it hundreds of times. Another founder from the Middle East told me, "What moved our startup forward wasn't capital. It was one key introduction that opened the first ten doors." They understood that they needed to adapt to the local culture, which heavily relies on relationships and building trust before attempting to sell anything. And this is when they began to achieve success.

Another tech leader told me that being a connector isn't about knowing everyone; it's about connecting people. It's about recognizing who needs each other before they do, and immersing yourself in a mission to connect people for the benefit of everyone around you. One easy way to do this is to introduce someone in your network to someone else. Believe me, when you do, you will feel a great sense of fulfillment.

Another thing I can leave you with is that before deciding to scale to new geographies and regions, study the place. If you're able to travel there, do so. Spend a couple of days, or possibly a week or two, to gain a deeper understanding. Talk to the locals and those involved in business there, and learn from them how things are done. Also, scale one region at a time because if you try to do more, you might end up creating a lot of confusion, which would cause a slowdown instead of a scaling operation. Though connections are global, the execution is always local.

CHAPTER 7

Real Mentorship, Real Impact

How many times have you seen this title on business cards or LinkedIn profiles: "Trusted Advisor"? This is a title that, unfortunately, has become somewhat of a cliché in our time.

The word "advisor" actually takes us back to the past, to a moment when people wanted someone more senior than themselves giving them advice on how to do things the right way, based, of course, on their experience. I am fortunate enough to have a couple of genuine individuals who I consider mentors. And the reason why I call them that is that these are the people who keep me accountable for what I'm doing.

I've had them in different stages of my life. At one point, I had people trying to help me figure out what I wanted to do with my career. At another, I had people advising me on how I should be communicating.

Today, I still have mentors—not people I hire, but people I trust and who I can keep close to me. They question me and hold me accountable. This is something I also try to do, giving back to the people I meet.

What frustrates me is that fake titles, such as "trusted advisor" and "mentor," are really detrimental to the new generation. We seek genuine individuals who can bring genuine value. We need people who can understand not only business, not only technology, but also how they can emotionally and psychologically help people who are starting their own companies.

People often confuse advice with mentorship. Advice is when you are faced with a choice and ask people what they think. They can advise you to go this route or that route. So, you get someone to advise you on, for example, which color best fits your brand. Alternatively, you might consider bringing in someone to advise you on which technology is better suited to your needs.

Mentorship, on the other hand, is long-term. Mentors don't just do the job and leave you. They become your friends. They are the people who really care about you. They get you back on track if you start to do things the wrong way. Mentors are very important, especially in the early stages of running a business or when you are doing it for the first time.

With all the advancements in technology, we are currently in an age where anyone can start a business. However, running a business requires more than just taking an idea, building it, and presenting it to people. You need to acquire a wide range of skills. You need someone to mentor you, to stay with you over the long term. And you might need more than one. It depends on your experience.

You may need someone who will mentor you on the best way to go and how to tell your story, as we saw in the previous chapters. You may need someone to mentor you on how to stay grounded so you don't continue to show off. You may need a mentor who will continually question your vision and keep you on track to achieve the goal you have set for yourself.

I've seen this on the podcast because I've had many true mentors, and I've observed the way they handle things. You can spot these guys from very far distances. They know how to establish a bond between their mentees and themselves. They don't immediately jump on everything related to business. They try to build trust first. They try to build the relationship first. To do this, they ask a lot of questions instead of just waiting for you to ask them questions. When you encounter such people, you need to work with them. You need to see what they do.

The best mentors are those who allow you to observe how they do things. If you're lucky and have someone who's a titan in the business, you should ask them to allow you to spend a day with them and observe how they interact with people, how they treat their employees, how they make decisions, and how they behave in times of crisis. This is very important. You want to walk alongside these people.

Now, if I want to put things on the other side of the table, not everyone is ready to be a mentee—and this is normal. It's an evolution because not everyone I meet, especially from Gen Z (which I have big hopes for), is ready to be mentored.

When you're young, you want to prove to the world that you will be the best. You will be the best business owner. You will be the best developer. You will be the best marketer. You will be the best sales guy ever. Initially, I tend to allow these people to make mistakes. The reason I do this is that if you don't allow people to make mistakes, they will never learn from them. If we continue to give them, as mentioned in the previous chapters, ready-made blueprints and step-by-step guides, telling them, "Hey, this is what you want to do," they will fail.

I can tell when someone is ready to be mentored because they start asking questions. Another indicator is that they begin to take calculated risks, not putting themselves in too much danger. They also admit it when they do something wrong.

It's challenging to work with individuals who have large egos. This is why it is essential to understand that when a mentor evaluates someone, there are a few key things they will be observing. First of all, you need to control your ego. You need to admit that you can make mistakes, so the potential mentor can see that you are grounded. You need to be curious. You need to master the ability to convey your passion and determination to the outside world. You want the mentor to say, "This guy is up to something, and I want to mentor them so they can reach the next level."

You should possess these qualities before asking for help from a mentor, because if you ask in an arrogant way, it suggests that you're not grounded and that you have an attitude. You would have better luck with the so-called advisors, but not with the mentors.

I have been fortunate to speak with many founders and mentors on the podcast. Many of them have told me that the best advice they got wasn't just advice. It was a mentor asking them a question that changed their perspective.

One guest told me that mentorship isn't about having all the answers. It's about creating a space where someone feels brave enough to find their own. Another shared that it's real mentorship when the person still checks in long after the pitch is over.

Now, if you want to be a successful mentor, you need, first of all, to be authentic. You also need to offer real, specific value, and you need to do this without asking for anything in return. Believe me, if you choose the right mentee, you will be compensated in other ways.

I believe true mentorship is transformational. It's not transactional. It's not like you pay for one hour to speak to someone and then it ends. This is advice, paid advice, but real mentors are people who stay with you and try to transform how you are doing things today.

I have an interesting story about a mentor who worked with one of the very large platforms, Twitch, actually. He mentored the CEO, and he told me that the CEO was very worried about his team not feeling connected to each other, as it was during the COVID pandemic. The mentor discussed psychology with the CEO and provided him with advice on understanding how people behave in similar times to the pandemic.

Then, they worked together on a formula that allowed them to maintain a sense of connection, even though they were geographically separated within the U.S. Some of them were even based in Europe. They did something very similar to gathering around a campfire, but they did it virtually.

When they implemented this, the morale and productivity of the company's employees increased significantly. Later on, when the pandemic was over, they made it a kind of tradition, and they continue to do it every quarter. So, they get together and call it the Campfire Gathering.

This is a story where the mentor had known the founder for a long time, even before he started the company. They stayed friends, and they always remember this moment because, when the CEO was feeling lost, the mentor was able to offer not only words of support but also something more meaningful. They brainstormed together and came up with a lasting solution.

When it comes to finding a mentor, it's best to have a warm introduction. This is the ideal approach. Build the relationship. At the very least, allow the mentor to observe what you're doing for some time.

Some people simply call themselves mentors and put themselves out there, which is fine. I don't mind it when someone reaches out to me out of the blue, as long as they are genuine and not just using a template with a different name each time they send it, if you get what I mean.

As you may have figured out by now, Steve Jobs is somewhat of an idol of mine, so I often quote him. He mentioned in one of his interviews that the only thing you need to do is speak to people. He gave the example of how, when he wanted something, he called one of the owners of HP, and ended up getting a job there. Sometimes, as a founder or entrepreneur, you need to take the leap and reach out to people, but you must do it authentically.

Don't just make things up. Be who you are. Reach out to people and say, "Hey, I need help. Can you help me?" You'll be surprised by the response that you get.

CHAPTER 8

Silicon Valley Lessons and Global Adoption

Since childhood, I have been fascinated by the stories I read about Silicon Valley in magazines and books. It's like that mysterious place where all the cool technology comes from.

I always dreamed that one day I would either work there or with someone from there. I was fortunate enough to work with founders from Silicon Valley and get hands-on experience with technologies originating from there. However, I have always been curious as to what the Valley's secret sauce is.

To find out what makes startups from there so successful, I began exploring what others had to say about the Valley. Some people said, "It's because money is abundant there." Others said, "They're just lucky." No matter the reason, people thought that they could replicate that success by copying a few things, without understanding what the real ingredients that made it work were, what made the Valley, "the Valley."

I'm mentioning this because I know many people share the ambition to build an ecosystem similar to the one in Silicon Valley. If you're in the Valley, that's good for you. If you're not, perhaps this will help you consider what it takes to be successful.

There's a famous saying that "geography is destiny," which is somewhat true. However, if we really look at history, location matters, but it's in our hands to see how we can change. What people see in Silicon Valley is a finalized product. They forget how all these things came together to make the Valley, "the Valley." There were multiple ingredients.

The first reason Silicon Valley flourished was that it had freedom of thought. I don't mean this from a political or religious perspective. Instead, I mean the freedom to dream big, without any limits. This is what's called the first principle: to always say, "Maybe it's possible to do this. Maybe it's possible to achieve that." This is the first thing that makes a startup founder succeed. You need to believe that you can achieve anything. Even if it seems impossible, you still need to try until you are proven wrong.

The second reason the Valley became the Valley is the very famous philosophy: "fail fast and fail often." I don't have the word "failure" in my dictionary. I don't believe that someone fails in the sense that you fail in English, although I'm not a native English speaker; however, it's very close to the word "fall." This is why I see failing as a stepping stone. It's not that you have failed. You're not someone who should be looked at as taboo.

Failing is actually a lesson. It's a blessing because, as Edison said, if you're not trying enough, it means you're not trying at all. This is where a culture of actually pushing people to make mistakes, learn from them quickly, and then pivot emerges. This is also a big part of what made the Valley, the Valley.

The third key ingredient in Silicon Valley's rise was the collaboration between academia and industry, with Stanford University at its heart. In the 1950s, Stanford's dean of engineering, Frederick Terman, encouraged faculty and students to work with local businesses. He leased university land to create Stanford Industrial Park, attracting companies like Hewlett-Packard, founded by Stanford alumni Bill Hewlett and David Packard. Terman also supported research in semiconductors, which led to breakthroughs by scientists like William Shockley, whose work sparked the growth of firms like Fairchild Semiconductor and Intel. This synergy, where universities share knowledge, talent, and resources with industry, creates a flywheel of innovation that other regions can emulate by fostering similar partnerships.

Today, regions like Dubai or Singapore can replicate this by encouraging universities to collaborate with startups, offering incubators, or funding joint research. It's not about copying Silicon Valley but creating local ecosystems where ideas flow freely between classrooms and boardrooms.

I have also noticed that founders in the Valley are relentlessly obsessed with making their ideas their main focus. They eat, drink, and breathe their ideas, and they are very passionate about them. They don't talk about anything else. This mindset enables founders in any ecosystem to successfully build their startups.

The last ingredient of Silicon Valley's success is capital. Nothing can succeed without capital. This is usually what people see in the Valley today. This last ingredient complements all the others mentioned above.

Now, having studied this and having had the chance to visit the Valley multiple times in my career, it has given me clarity on what makes a good technology. Usually, we only talk about the Valley's success stories. No one talks about the companies that fail. However, there's nothing wrong with making mistakes, with starting something and failing miserably at it. This is where things start to change.

Here's how I spot promising technologies and judge whether a startup might become something significant. First, the founding team is crucial. As an entrepreneur, you need to be passionate about what you are building. You need to have a clear purpose, which we discussed in the first chapter. You need to show the world that this is your mission. This is why you are living your life on this earth. When I see people like that, I say, "I know that they're going to succeed one way or another."

Second, I know that the technology is promising when it creates what is called the "network effect." A network effect in the business world occurs when someone builds something, people start to use it, and those users begin to recommend it to others. You need to build something that everyone wants and recommends to each other.

You might be saying, "But this is only in B2C," or business-to-consumer businesses. No, it's also doable in B2B. If you can build a community, cultivate evangelists, and attract early adopters, you'll be successful.

Here's another way that I spot promising technologies: they come at the right time to the right market. We've often seen where awesome technologies came too early to the market and no one adopted them. To address this, founders need to articulate their value proposition clearly, explaining why they are in the right time and place, and build a network effect around themselves.

As I said, founders also need to be passionate. They need to be risk-takers and visionaries. They also need to be flexible and able to pivot at any point in time. It doesn't matter if they didn't have any experience before. People often think that only experienced individuals can build successful startups, but that's not true. If you have the will and your mission, you will succeed.

Now, the thing is, when we talk about Silicon Valley and try to take the same model globally, it's the people who idealize the valley blindly who fail. People need to follow their own path. Simply taking something and imitating it in another place doesn't necessarily work. There's a danger here because, if we copy blindly, we might not see the same results.

This is where people say, "Hey, the Valley is a failure for us." It's not a failure. It's just that, sometimes, you need to adapt the Valley version to your location, you need to prepare the ecosystem first, or both. I've seen this in the region where I live, the Middle East, in Dubai.

Many have tried, including myself, to copy what people do in the Valley and have failed. The reason is that we were not ready. We didn't have the same ecosystem. If the ecosystem isn't there, you need to find a way to build it.

Now, you might be asking, "How can I build an ecosystem if I'm alone at the beginning?" Well, you start educating people. You start telling people success stories. You try to see how you can apply the same concept, but localize it from a cultural perspective, or even from a language perspective. However, be cautious when copying a model to your location, as it may not function properly.

You may need to have a pre-prepared base. Think about it this way. Let's say you are able to relocate the Empire State Building to a sandy location, such as the beach. What will happen? It will fall. It will get destroyed. Why? Because you didn't build the proper infrastructure to support such a huge building on top of the sand. Therefore, you need to do some preparatory work, and the same principle applies when discussing the replication of Silicon Valley's model in other regions.

We've seen some locations that succeeded and some that are still struggling. One of the things that people often overlook is the freedom I was referring to—the way people are free to think without any limitations. If you don't have this completely in place, you will hit a wall.

I've learned a great deal about this topic from my podcast, on which I've interviewed guests from the East, West, and all around the globe.

One of these guests told me, "We treated Silicon Valley like gospel, and it nearly drained our business." What works there doesn't always land here, which is true. This is because you need to have your own story.

Another investor shared that the valley's real edge is in technology and its decision-making speed. That's what needs to be localized. Absolutely. I couldn't agree with him more regarding this. Yet another guest told me, "We didn't copy the Valley playbook; we copied their culture of urgency. That's what moved the needle." Again, the lesson here is that when you copy, copy the things that work, and then see how you can adapt them to your own location.

This is my actionable step for you. If you are building something and, like me, are fascinated by Silicon Valley, take one of the Valley things that worked and see if it exists in your market. If it doesn't, what do you have to do so people will accept your business and start to take you seriously? Whatever it is, this is the thing you need to do. If it doesn't exist, you need to start working on bringing it into existence. You might need to build your community first. You may need to put in a lot of work.

We tell people to move fast, but don't move fast without proper planning because greatness isn't a place; it's a replicable mindset.

CHAPTER 9

Looking Toward the Future

I couldn't end this book without discussing something that, at first glance, looks like a cliché: what I expect the future to bring. Now, I'm not a fortune teller, but as I mentioned in the previous chapter, I learned to spot some signals, and I hope that they will be a kind of guiding point for you.

As someone with a technology background, I have had the opportunity to work with various technology companies throughout my career. I currently do the same, investing in and supporting tech startups. However, we're living in very, very different times now. As of the writing of this book, mid-2025, artificial intelligence (AI) is taking the world by storm.

We are seeing a lot of new technologies emerging, and whether it's GenAI or other technologies, they are all exciting. What excites me the most about the next wave of technologies is not only how cool they are or how people will use them. I believe we have reached a moment in history where technology is enabling us to break through boundaries that we thought we couldn't cross.

We are in an era when technology is leading us to believe that we can achieve everything we want. Technology is empowering entrepreneurs to turn ideas into reality faster than ever. Consider how AI tools, like no-code platforms, let you build a prototype in days, not months, or how cloud computing allows solo founders to scale globally without massive upfront costs. When I started my podcast, affordable recording software and distribution platforms made it possible to reach thousands with minimal resources. This speed and accessibility mean that your vision—no matter how bold—can become tangible with the right tools and hustle.

It's exciting for humanity to break new boundaries with this technology, making our lives much easier. Considering how our ancestors lived and the suffering they endured to survive, we should be grateful for the waves of technology that have emerged.

People often only think about the generative aspects of AI and the tools that we use to generate text, images, and videos, which is awesome, but AI, machine learning, and other technologies like quantum computing, space technologies, medical technologies, IoT, you name it, are allowing us not only to make our lives easier, but to also cure diseases faster.

They are allowing our kids to learn faster. They are allowing everyone on earth to be better educated, and I'm not talking here about education as a degree, but rather about everyone becoming aware of the concepts that humanity has accumulated over the years. This is truly exciting because, with technologies like large language models, we now have the knowledge of humanity, spanning thousands of years, at our fingertips.

Imagine what we can do with the combination of these technologies that are coming, whether it's blockchain or quantum computing. I'm a big believer that we'll reach a point where we'll have less stressful lives, and I'm hoping that we'll also hear fewer stories about burnout and its associated issues. Technology is allowing us, for the first time, to dream of a life where we can truly enjoy our moments on this planet. Remember, even though our time on this earth may seem very long, we actually live a relatively short span of time.

People ask me, "Are you worried about all these new waves of emerging technologies?" To be honest, I am not, and the reason I am not worried is that history has shown us that every time a new technology emerges, some people will inevitably try to use it for malicious purposes. Think about fire. Fire was a big discovery at some stage, but almost certainly, some people argued that because fire can burn us, we should not use it.

As we embrace AI and emerging technologies, entrepreneurs must navigate ethical challenges to build trust and create a lasting impact. For example, AI systems can unintentionally perpetuate biases if trained on flawed data, as seen in early facial recognition tools that struggled with diverse skin tones. To counter this, founders should prioritize diverse teams, transparent algorithms, and user feedback to ensure fairness.

Privacy is another concern—customers want to know their data is safe. Startups like those building blockchain-based identity solutions are tackling this issue by giving users control over their own data. By addressing these issues early, you not only avoid pitfalls but also differentiate your brand as one that cares about doing good.

Now, when it comes to entrepreneurship, it, too, is undergoing rapid change. Back in the day, maybe thirty or forty years ago, people thought that entrepreneurs were dropout kids sitting in a garage or their dorm rooms, building something, and they needed to have a lot of determination and resources to build successful businesses.

Nowadays, everyone talks about how it would be easy to have more entrepreneurs in society, but the fact is, entrepreneurs will need to be prepared for the future as well. They need to continuously learn, adapt to the latest changes, and also consider how to refine their models.

Now, they can't just be offering a technical difference. Entrepreneurs need to tell their stories so they can differentiate themselves from the rest of the pack. They need to learn about personal branding. They need to learn more about how to stay authentic while also shining in front of their audience. They need to be ready to be disrupted. Previously, disruptions occurred every decade, sometimes even more frequently. However, with the rise of AI, especially in the past three or four years, we're now seeing startups being started and then shuttered within a year.

When you start a business, you must think carefully about how you will respond to disruptions so that, when they occur, you remain resilient to them. You need to determine how to build this business so that even in the face of these headwinds, you can remain strong and not give up. You need to prepare.

Disruption is the new norm. You need to prepare for it with your team, with your culture, with your passion and determination. This is yet another reason why purpose is essential.

What kind of legacy do you want to leave behind? How do you want people to remember you? This is why you need to avoid the shiny things, as well as the dooms and glooms. You need to build businesses that people will remember: "Yeah, this is the founder who successfully built a business that helped people."

This is the mission you should be after, and it's why I have a mission. I shifted from being a technologist to a consultant and then to a business operator. To leave a lasting legacy, I aim to bridge the innovation gaps by supporting fellow startups. This is why I decided to establish an investment fund that bridges regional gaps and enables more entrepreneurs to succeed. I want the world to be a better place than how I found it.

I know it's a cliché, but it's the truth. The people with this mentality are the ones who will actually move humanity forward. This is why I talk so much about passion, mission, and determination.

Now, going back to what I learned recently from my discussions on the podcast, one founder building an AI told me, "Everyone's excited about the tech, but I'm more focused on what happens when people aren't ready for it."

This sparked a thought: *When we decide to build something, we need to make sure that people are ready to use it, especially if it's a new technology.* This is where we also need to learn and teach others about how things should move smoothly when it comes to emerging technology, and always accept the fact that people might initially reject it. That means you'll have a few early adopters, and then the masses will follow, and you need to execute on this sharply.

A deep-tech founder told me, "We"e not preparing for the next twelve months. We're designing for five years out." The biggest risk is building for the wrong timeline, which is exactly what we discussed in the previous chapter.

You need to see the full journey. You need to be able to take people from where they are today and show them the future. When we look to the future, we need to see the journey in its entirety before we embark. Think about it like when you decide to go from one place to another. You open your navigation app, and it shows you the entire path, even offering alternative routes.

Another founder once told me that you don't build the future by guessing. You build it by learning faster than it arrives. Again, we need to be careful to learn quickly. As I mentioned in the previous chapter, one of the key values is that you build fast and fail fast. You need to do both things.

Here's how you can determine if you're prepared for the future. Imagine three things that are happening now, and then imagine how they will be in three years. How will they impact your business, and how will you react? Look at the worst-case scenario, and try to see how you can build on top of it. Just remember, legacy is built by those who prepare, adapt, and empower others.

Legacy in Motion

I f you've made it this far in the book, thank you very much, because it appears I've been able to take you with me on this journey that I've tried to simulate for you. My mission is to empower entrepreneurs like you to make a positive impact on the world. By connecting, sharing, and learning together, we can create a legacy that outlives us all.

With my story and the lessons I've learned from almost five hundred episodes of podcasting, I hope I kept you engaged and provided you with some great takeaways. Here are several key points that I want you to remember from this book.

1. **You must start with your purpose.** We discussed the importance of purpose many times, but the main thing is that you need to do your homework and find what you're passionate about, why you exist on this planet, and why you're here. So, do the work and identify that before you do anything else.

2. **It's important to have a visionary mindset.** Don't just think about today. Think about where you want to be in five years.

Don't just think about how you can build a business that lasts for the next funding round. Think about building one that will last for generations to come.

3. It's necessary to accept that sometimes **you need to step outside your comfort zone**, which means taking bold actions and making difficult decisions. Live as if there's no tomorrow.

4. I want you to recognize that **you need to create your own success formula**. No one is going to give you a cheat sheet that you can simply apply to find success. You need to build your own success strategies. You need to become the source of inspiration for your own success. There are no shortcuts. There is only inspiration and passion.

5. **Don't ignore building your personal brand,** especially in these times. Nowadays, people want to see the faces behind the ideas and businesses they support. They want to understand why you are doing what you do. You need to be ready to tell your story. This is why you need to be authentic. You need to show empathy and put yourself in your customer's shoes to succeed.

6. It's important to **remember that geography might be a *destiny*,** but you can't change it. When you move from one geographical area to another, you need to understand the cultural nuances while maintaining a global perspective.

7. **Look for mentors who care about you,** and don't be tricked by advisors who use clickbait to show you that they can help you.

Remember, as we mentioned earlier, think about transformation, not transaction. Surrounding yourself with mentors will lead to success.

8. **Learn to spot signals and understand how you can succeed** even if you are not in the best ecosystems in the world for a startup. You can create your own greatness by building your community and understanding how to take pre-existing ideas and add your own touch to them, even if you are outside of Silicon Valley. We've seen people who succeeded at this, so there's nothing that can stop you from being a builder at a Silicon Valley level, even if you are not living there.

As you close this book, reflect on the legacy you want to build—a business that solves a real problem, a community that thrives, or a story that inspires others. Start today: write down one action you'll take this week to move toward that vision, whether it's drafting your purpose statement or reaching out to a mentor. My podcast journey taught me that taking small, purposeful steps can lead to a significant impact. Keep building, and let's connect to shape a better future together.

I would like to invite you to continue the conversation. If you're building a startup, creating something that could change lives, or developing something with a purpose, and you have a unique perspective on the world, I'd like to connect with you (scan the QR code at the beginning or end of this book). You can also tune in to my podcast, *The CTO Show with Mehmet*, where I share more stories and insights from founders worldwide—available on all major platforms.

THANK YOU FOR READING MY BOOK!

I WOULD LOVE TO CONNECT!

If this book sparked something in you, share your story with me. I'd love to hear about the purpose that drives you and the legacy you're building. Better yet, join our growing community of entrepreneurs where we support one another in turning dreams into reality. Let's build something extraordinary together.

Scan the QR Code:

I appreciate your interest in my book and value your feedback, as it helps me improve future versions. I would appreciate it if you could leave your invaluable review on Amazon.com with your feedback.
Thank you!

www.ingramcontent.com/pod-product-compliance
Lightning Source LLC
Chambersburg PA
CBHW070941210326
41520CB00021B/7004